THE IMAGINEER

For Charles, Evan and Felix
—three amazing imagineers. CC

For Vincenzo. LM

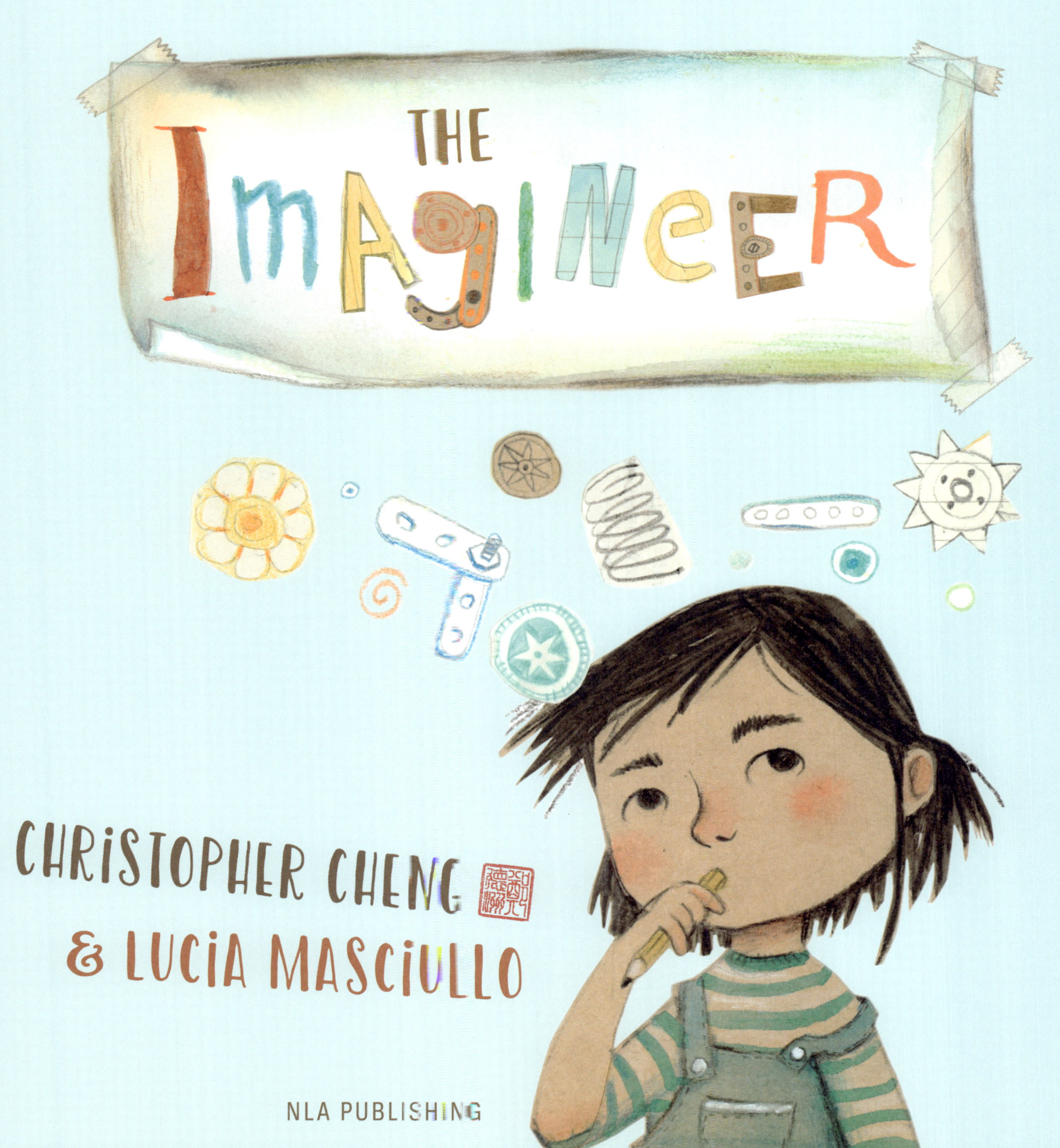

CHRISTOPHER CHENG

& LUCIA MASCIULLO

NLA PUBLISHING

Penny was an IMAGINEER.

She imagined with her mind and then created with her hands.

She loved to pull things apart and put them back together again. She twisted and turned, screwed and tied, taped and stacked and covered.

If her creations didn't work out the first time, she'd start all over again.

She imagined her spaceship
with interstellar communicator
shooting far into space...

...and her submarine with aquasonic visualiser exploring the deepest oceans.

She sketched and planned and scribbled.

Penny's imagination was massive.
But her apartment was miniscule.

Grandpa lived in an enormous house a long, long way away. So when Penny went to visit for the very first time, and discovered rooms packed with all kinds of stuff, she was flabbergasted.

She talked on a telephone that was hanging on the wall and she sliced potatoes with Grandpa's wartime mandolin.

She sang at the organ while Grandpa pumped the bellows.

She turned a handle to churn homemade butter until her arms cried, 'Stop!'

'Everything has a purpose. Everything has a job to do,' said Grandpa.

Then Penny discovered the shed.

She could barely breathe.

Particulars of oth
No. 1291.
Coffee or Spice Mills, wi
or fine grinding

Penny couldn't work out what many of the bits and pieces were used for, no matter how long she investigated them.

But Grandpa knew.

And Penny was sure that these thingamajigs and whatchamacallits and fandangled contraptions (which is what Grandpa called anything he had forgotten the name of) would be useful.

For a long while Penny sat, and pondered,
and wondered what she could build...

No. 1377.
PAT. JUNE 5.88

No. 1288.

And then it was ready—Penny's most wonderful, phantasmagorical, incredibleacious, stupendorific creation... just for Grandpa!

CHRISTOPHER CHENG

Within the walls of an old inner-city Sydney terrace filled with loads of books dwells Christopher Cheng. A teacher by profession, he is Co-chair of the International Advisory Board for SCBWI and the author of many children's books, including his previous NLA Publishing title, *New Year Surprise!*, illustrated by Di Wu. Christopher has always loved to write (and mostly always carries his notebook and pens) but he never thought he would be a full-time children's author. When his wife Bini first showed him her father's wartime mandolin, he said, 'What is it?' and the seed for this story began germinating.
www.chrischeng.com

LUCIA MASCIULLO

Lucia is an award-winning illustrator who loves to illustrate children's books. Born and bred in Livorno, Italy, she moved to Australia in 2007 and since then she has illustrated more than 20 books, including the CBCA Honour Book and Prime Minister's Awards shortlisted *Come Down, Cat!* by Sonya Hartnett and the *Olive of Groves* trilogy by Katrina Nannestad. She now lives on the Gold Coast. Lucia likes to create whimsical characters and she works mainly with traditional techniques, mixing watercolour, pencil and collage.
www.luciamasciullo.com

Carpet sweeper

Before electric suction vacuum cleaners, carpet sweepers would be pushed or pulled over carpet or floors and waste was swept into canisters by the brush bristles, a bit like a broom.

Butter churn

Churns transformed cream into butter. Turning the handle on the outside moved paddles or plungers inside the container, churning the cream until it turned into butter.

Sad iron

Sad irons were made of solid metal and heated on a stove. They were heavy so that they could smooth out the wrinkles in clothes—this also meant they made good doorstops. The handles were sometimes made with wood, but if the handle was also metal, it was wrapped with a cloth before it was picked up. 'Sad' is an old word for 'solid'.

Kerosene lamp

These lamps were fuelled by kerosene in the base. They were used to create light before electricity, like a long-burning candle. To protect the user from the flame, and stop the flame blowing out, it was covered with a glass chimney.

Coffee grinder

Green coffee beans were roasted and then poured into a small cup. These were then ground by turning a handle at the top of the mill. The ground beans were collected in a drawer at the base of the mill to make fresh coffee.

TOOLS FOR IMAGINEERING

Telephone

When they weren't being used, telephone headpieces were hung from hooks on wall boxes. These boxes connected to wires that ran outside the house to the telephone lines. These lines transmitted voices and sounds to other buildings.

Mandolin

Mandolins were used for evenly slicing long thin strips of vegetables (and sometimes fruit). There were two different blades which meant that the vegetable strips could either be made straight or crinkle cut. This one was purchased in a European market soon after the Second World War.

Fruit juicer

Fruit juicers were clamped to a bench, like peelers. Turning the handle squeezed juice from the fruit into the container below. The pulp and seeds fell into another container.

Reed organ

Reed organs (commonly known as pump organs) made music for many homes and small churches. By alternately pressing the left and right pedals, air was pumped through the bellows. When a key on the keyboard was pressed while the feet pedalled, the brass reeds vibrated to create sound.

Hand push mower

A hand push mower was pushed (or pulled) back and forth across a lawn to cut the grass.

Metal basin

Metal basins were used to hold water for washing clothes, or to collect wood or any odds and ends that would fit inside.

Milk can

Milk cans, or churns, were used to transport milk from dairies (where cows were milked) to the cooperative, where milk from many farms was collected.

Cylinder record

To play music, a cylinder with sound recorded on it was placed into a machine called a phonograph. The phonograph's needle would be lowered to rest on the cylinder. By rotating the phonograph's crank (its handle), the cylinder would turn under the needle, reading the music and sending it out through the large horn.

Kettle

Before we had electric kettles to heat water, there were stove-top kettles. They had a spout, lid and a handle on top. When water boiled, steam was created. If the kettle had a steam whistle, the steam escaping through the whistle signalled that the water had boiled. Some people still use stove-top kettles.

Yashica camera

To take photographs with this Yashica camera, the photographer looked through the viewfinder at the top to make sure the lens was pointed at their subject. They then pressed the shutter to expose the film to light. To see the printed picture, the film had to be developed in a darkroom using chemicals.

LIST OF IMAGES

Mrs Potts' Crown Sad Irons, illustration on page 537 in *Anthony Hordern and Sons Catalogue*, (Sydney: Anthony Hordern and Sons, 1907), nla.cat-vn584747

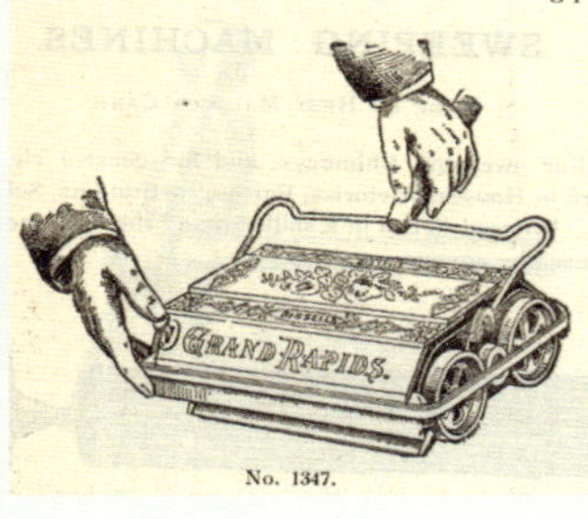

Bissell's Grand Rapid Carpet Sweeper, illustration on page 537 in *Anthony Hordern and Sons Catalogue* (Sydney: Anthony Hordern and Sons, 1907), nla.cat-vn584747

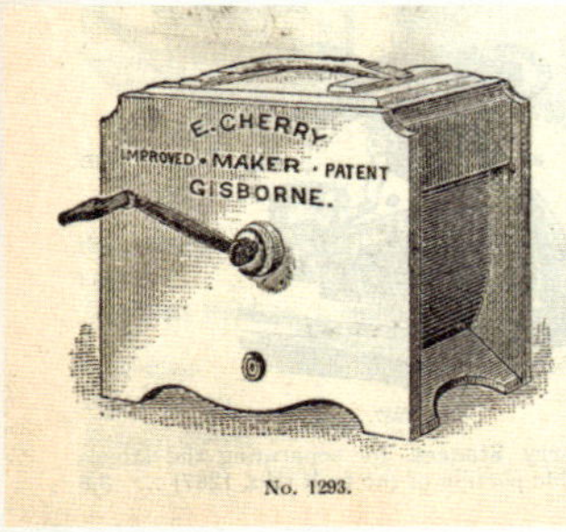

Improved Bentwood Churns, No. 1293, illustration on page 528 in *Anthony Hordern and Sons Catalogue* (Sydney: Anthony Hordern and Sons, 1907), nla.cat-vn584747

A Woman at an Office Desk Surrounded by Lamps and Wearing a Coat, Due to the Effects of the Coal Miner's Strike, Mayfield, New South Wales, 1949, nla.cat-vn8035711

Square Box Coffee Mills, illustration on page 528 in *Anthony Hordern and Sons Catalogue* (Sydney: Anthony Hordern and Sons, 1907), nla.cat-vn584747

Electric Telephone, illustration on page 47 in *The Australasian Ironmonger, Engineer and Metalworker: A Strictly Intercolonial Journal*, 1 December 1890, (Melbourne: Australasian Ironmonger, 1890–1900), nla.cat-vn1158236

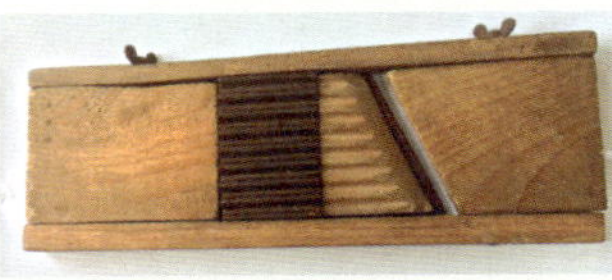

Mandolin, c.1945, courtesy Christopher Cheng

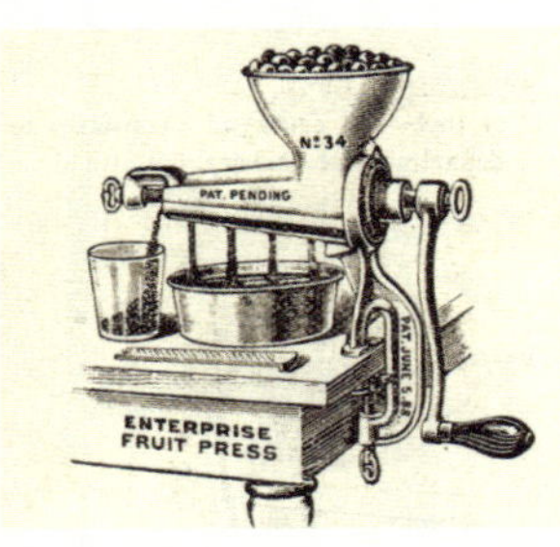

Enterprise Fruit, Wine and Jelly Presses, illustration on page 528 in *Anthony Hordern and Sons Catalogue* (Sydney: Anthony Hordern and Sons, 1907), nla.cat-vn584747

Wes Stacey, *Interior Room of Kings Plains Homestead, Glen Innes, New South Wales* (detail), c.1970, nla.cat-vn5158066

Trish Ainslie, *Doreen Cassidy Helping with the Weekly Wash*, 2002, nla.cat-vn88922, courtesy Trish Ainslie and Roger Garwood

Michael Terry, *Elderly Man Identified as Wilson Standing Outside with Garden Tools, England*, c.1918, nla.cat-vn7004286

Jim Fitzpatrick, *Milk Carrier Frederick (Fred) Jones Delivers Full Milk Cans at Drouin's Co-operative Milk Factory, Drouin, Victoria*, c.1944, nla.cat-vn2172484

Edison Cylinder Records Surrounding Phonographs in a Sound Room at the Nicholson and Company Music Store, Sydney, c.1905, nla.cat-vn4777400

The Sydney Morning Herald, *Stove on the Yacht Gullmarn with a Kettle and Stand, Sydney Harbour*, c.1932, nla.cat-vn6217633, courtesy Fairfax Syndication, fairfaxsyndication.com

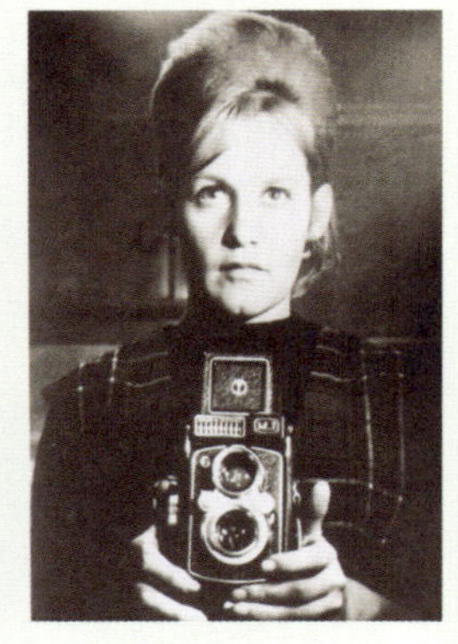

Sue Ford, *Self Portrait of Sue Ford*, 1961, nla.cat-vn1967261

The Sydney Morning Herald, *Sydney Morning Herald Staff Members Using Typewriter and a Telephone, New South Wales*, c.1920, nla.cat-vn6342364, courtesy Fairfax Syndication, fairfaxsyndication.com

Juno Gemes, *Robert Harris's Desk, Glebe, Sydney*, 1993, nla.cat-vn5895309

House Fire Engine, illustration on page 74 in *The Australasian Ironmonger, Engineer and Metalworker: A Strictly Intercolonial Journal*, 1 February 1890, (Melbourne: Australasian Ironmonger, 1890–1900), nla.cat-vn1158236

Alexander Collingridge, *Dame Enid Lyons Using a Treadle Sewing Machine*, c.1930, nla.cat-vn1517475

Fruit and Potato Peelers, illustration on page 528 in *Anthony Hordern and Sons Catalogue* (Sydney: Anthony Hordern and Sons, 1907), nla.cat-vn584747

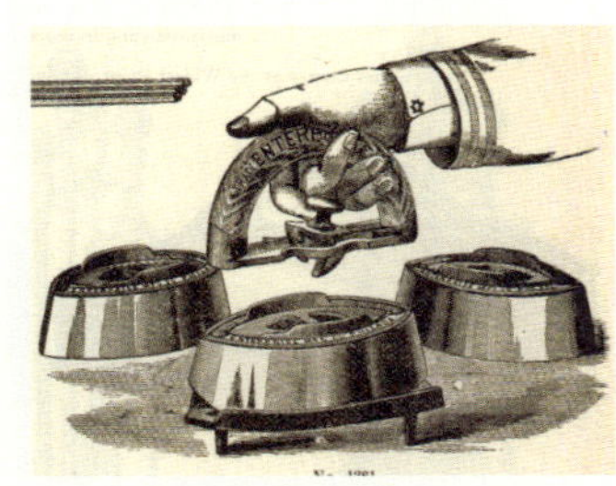

George Salter & Co… Sad Iron, illustration on page 87 in *The Australasian Ironmonger, Engineer and Metalworker: A Strictly Intercolonial Journal,* 1 December 1890 (Melbourne: Australasian Ironmonger, 1890–1900), nla.cat-vn1158236

Laundry Scrubs, illustration on page 536 in *Anthony Hordern and Sons Catalogue* (Sydney: Anthony Hordern and Sons, 1907), nla.cat-vn584747

Arthur William Emmerton, *Pram*, c.1915, nla.cat-vn3697235

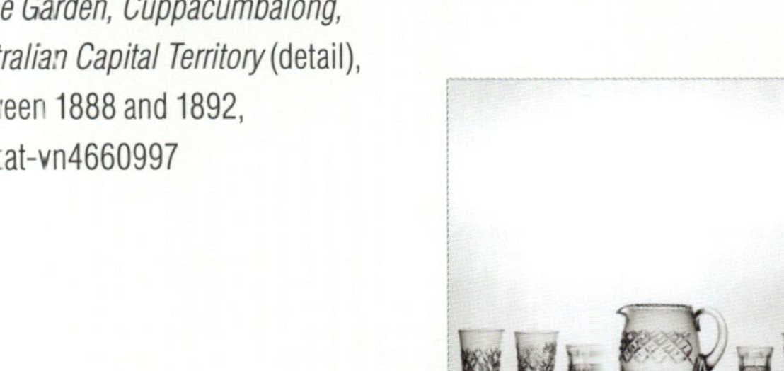

Rodolph De Salis Riding a Tricycle in the Garden, Cuppacumbalong, Australian Capital Territory (detail), between 1888 and 1892, nla.cat-vn4660997

Wolfgang Sievers, *Presentation Cup for Craven Print and Pack Importers of German M.A.N. Ausburg Printing Presses, Moorabbin, Victoria*, 1986, nla.cat-vn4314425

Bruce Howard, *Clock Showing Tram Departure Time for the South Pacific Electric Railway, at the Sydney Tramway Museum*, c.1976, nla.cat-vn778448

Wolfgang Sievers, *Crystal Jug and Glassware Produced by ACI Sydney*, 1981, nla.cat-vn1035605

Grace Lucas Weighing a Baby Koala Mannagum at Koala Park, West Pennant Hills, New South Wales, 1931, nla.cat-vn6291540, courtesy Fairfax Syndication, fairfaxsyndication.com

Nash-Boothby Studios, *Chair with Fabric Upholstery, Government House, Canberra*, 1927, nla.cat-vn3119877

Stewart Dawson & Company, *Fob Watch Belonging to Henry Lawson*, c.1902, nla.cat.vn2124380

Published by National Library of Australia Publishing
Canberra ACT 2600

ISBN: 9781922507341

The National Library of Australia acknowledges Australia's First Nations Peoples—the First Australians—as the Traditional Owners and Custodians of this land and gives respect to the Elders—past and present—and through them to all Australian Aboriginal and Torres Strait Islander people.

Editor: Irma Gold
Printed in China by Everbest Printing Co. Ltd on FSC®-certified paper.

Find out more about NLA Publishing at library.gov.au/nla-publishing.

A catalogue record for this book is available from the National Library of Australia.